T0021763

POCKET STUDY SKILLS

*Series Editor: **Kate Williams**, Oxford Brookes University, UK*
Illustrations by Sallie Godwin

For the time-pushed student, the *Pocket Study Skills* pack a lot of advice into a little book. Each guide focuses on a single crucial aspect of study giving you step-by-step guidance, handy tips and clear advice on how to approach the important areas which will continually be at the core of your studies.

Published

14 Days to Exam Success (2nd edn)
Analyzing a Case Study
Blogs, Wikis, Podcasts and More
Brilliant Writing Tips for Students
Completing Your PhD
Doing Research (2nd edn)
Getting Critical (3rd edn)
How to Analyze Data
Managing Stress
Planning Your Dissertation (2nd edn)
Planning Your Essay (3rd edn)
Planning Your PhD
Posters and Presentations

Reading and Making Notes (2nd edn)
Referencing and Understanding Plagiarism (2nd edn)
Reflective Writing (2nd edn)
Report Writing (2nd edn)
Science Study Skills
Studying with Dyslexia (2nd edn)
Success in Groupwork (2nd edn)
Successful Applications
Time Management
Using Feedback to Boost Your Grades
Where's Your Evidence?
Writing for University (3rd edn)

POCKET STUDY SKILLS
Michael Shoolbred & Helen Cooper

WHERE'S YOUR ARGUMENT?

How to present your academic argument in writing

Second Edition

BLOOMSBURY ACADEMIC
LONDON • NEW YORK • OXFORD • NEW DELHI • SYDNEY

BLOOMSBURY ACADEMIC
Bloomsbury Publishing Plc
50 Bedford Square, London, WC1B 3DP, UK
1385 Broadway, New York, NY 10018, USA
29 Earlsfort Terrace, Dublin 2, Ireland

BLOOMSBURY, BLOOMSBURY ACADEMIC and the Diana logo are trademarks of Bloomsbury Publishing Plc

First published in Great Britain 2016
This edition published 2022

Copyright © Helen Cooper and Michael Shoolbred 2022

The authors have asserted their rights under the Copyright, Designs and Patents Act, 1988, to be identified as authors of this work.

Cover design: eStudio Calamar

All rights reserved. No part of this publication may be reproduced or transmitted in any form or by any means, electronic or mechanical, including photocopying, recording, or any information storage or retrieval system, without prior permission in writing from the publishers.

Bloomsbury Publishing Plc does not have any control over, or responsibility for, any third-party websites referred to in or in this book. All internet addresses given in this book were correct at the time of going to press. The author and publisher regret any inconvenience caused if addresses have changed or sites have ceased to exist, but can accept no responsibility for any such changes.

A catalogue record for this book is available from the British Library.

ISBN: PB: 978-1-3509-3262-3
         ePDF: 978-1-3509-3264-7
         eBook: 978-1-3509-3263-0

Series: Pocket Study Skills

Typeset by Integra Software Services Pvt. Ltd.
Printed and bound in India

To find out more about our authors and books visit www.bloomsbury.com and sign up for our newsletters.

Contents

Acknowledgements

We would like to thank Ioana Cerasella Chis and Khembi Maynard for reading the manuscript and for their feedback. We also received great advice from Dr Vikki Burns, Dr Karin Bottom, David Maynard and Pete Dalton.

We have been very lucky to work with Kate Williams, the hawk-eyed and knowledgeable series editor, and Helen Caunce, our supportive commissioning editor at Bloomsbury Academic. Thanks also to Sallie Godwin, the illustrator, and to the efficient and helpful production team.

We'd like to acknowledge the research of Professor Ken Hyland and colleagues on academic voice. We also acknowledge academic authors Professors Inger Mewburn and Helen Sword, both of whose work made us think.

Finally, thank you to the many students we've taught, whose work we've marked and who have inspired us.

Helen Cooper and Michael Shoolbred

Introduction

Do any of these comments look familiar? You may have seen feedback like this on your essays and assignments.

But what exactly do comments like this mean?

What your tutor really wants is for you to *have something to say*. It may be that you have included lots of information about your topic, but that your essay needs a stronger perspective, or viewpoint, running through it, leading to a clear 'take-home' message for the reader.

Quite often, your assignment question won't actually use the word 'argument'. But some form of argument is almost always implied. For instance, if you are asked to 'evaluate', to 'consider the evidence', to 'make a comparison', or to 'discuss the benefits of', you are being asked to make an argument. In fact, a lot of academic writing simply assumes that you will construct an argument or case.

That doesn't mean it's easy! It can be challenging to present a perspective while sticking to academic conventions such as objectivity. This book will show you how to build a convincing academic argument based on thorough research. We will reveal techniques for communicating your argument to a reader, from planning a logical structure to conveying your ideas in precise language. The book follows the assignment-writing process from first steps to final edit, showing how you can develop and communicate your argument at each stage.

We will also show you how to ensure that you are presenting a nuanced argument to the marker – in other words, an argument that explores the complexity of your topic.

This is important because your lecturers care about your ideas, your thinking and understanding. They especially want to know how what you think relates to previous views and research in your subject area. It matters that you can think independently, but are aware of the value of what has gone before. We are all, as Charles Darwin wrote, 'standing on the shoulders of giants'!

In this book, we will refer to 'assignments' and 'essays', meaning any normal length piece of academic writing. But we will also give you examples from work-based assignments. Our advice can be applied across most kinds of academic writing.

Tutors tend to use the word 'argument' when they mean:

- **making a series of claims**
- **constructing a logical case**
- **presenting a point of view.**

Constructing a logical case means:

- having an **overall point of view**
- making a **series of points** to justify that point of view
- providing **evidence to support those points.**

An assignment is an invitation to put forward a thoughtful response to a question. You should:

- tell the reader what you want to say in answer to the question, and what they will take away from the essay
- help them to follow the logic of what you are arguing, step by step
- show that you have considered the topic in a nuanced and critical way, rather than appearing to be too simplistic
- convince the reader that your perspective is valid.

Your argument is not something that should be stuck on the end, nor sectioned off in one part of the essay. It is *your* unique response to the question, based on research, evidence and critical thinking.

What do I think?

1 Stages of the task

We will demonstrate how to build your argument at each stage of the assignment-writing process. This chapter, and the diagram over the page, give an overview of that process. You will find more information and advice about each stage as you progress through the book.

Understanding the task (Part 1)

Before building your response, you need to be clear what you are responding to, and what your reader (your tutor or marker) wants. An argument is a communication from writer to reader, within the confines of a specific task. So, begin by thinking about that task and what it requires. Your assignment question, assignment guidance and learning outcomes will help.

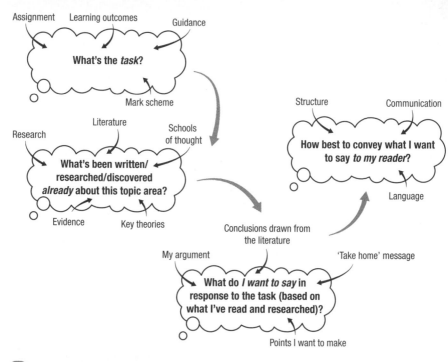

Assignment   Learning outcomes   Guidance

What's the *task*?

Mark scheme

Research   Literature   Schools of thought

What's been written/ researched/discovered *already* about this topic area?

Evidence   Key theories

Structure   Communication

How best to convey what I want to say *to my reader*?

Language

Conclusions drawn from the literature

My argument   'Take home' message

What do *I want to say* in response to the task (based on what I've read and researched)?

Points I want to make

Finding information and forming ideas (Part 2)

To argue effectively, you must become knowledgeable about your topic and familiar with key literature relating to it. *Your* perspective will emerge from reading critically and reviewing existing evidence. This is a key part of the process, and requires you to keep an open, inquisitive mind before you decide on your main argument.

Building your argument (Part 2)

Once you are well informed and have evaluated all the available evidence, you will be able to develop a response to your assignment question. You will ask yourself: *What does the evidence show? Now that I have explored the topic, what do I want to say about it?*

Planning and structuring (Part 3)

When you know what you want to argue, and why, it's time to think about how to communicate that to a reader. Set aside time between researching and writing to consider these important questions: *How best to present all my ideas to somebody who can't see inside my head? How can I guide them through my line of reasoning? What do I want to leave my reader thinking and feeling about this issue, and how can I achieve that?*

Writing (Parts 3 and 4)

Everything you do up to this point – considering the question, researching and planning – should make it easier to get your argument onto the page. The challenge is making sure the reader understands it and is convinced. You are writing for somebody else, showing them the relevance of your ideas and demonstrating why your perspective is valid.

Redrafting and editing (Part 5)

The redrafting and editing stage is all about the reader. You are making sure that your writing is clear, your transitions are smooth and the focus on the question is obvious throughout. Effective communication will ensure that your tutor never needs to ask 'where's your argument?'

It's important to plan your time so that you can research, structure, write and edit an effective argument. For more on planning timescales, see *Planning Your Essay* and *Time Management* in this series.

Next, find out how to get to grips with your task.

Although you're aiming to develop an individual response to your assignment question, remember that you are writing to a brief. A brilliant argument will only receive the mark it deserves if it answers the question, follows the guidance and meets the learning outcomes.

When thinking about how to approach your task, consider:

- the task words in your assignment question, e.g. 'discuss', 'evaluate', 'critically analyse' (For more on task words, see *Writing for University* in this series.)
- subject matter and what the question is asking you to do with it
- learning outcomes you are required to meet and the guidance that accompanies your assignment
- assessment criteria or marking scheme.

The assignment question

Here are some questions to ask yourself once you have been given, or have chosen, your assignment question:

- What is it actually asking me to do?
- What knowledge and skills should I be demonstrating?
- Do I understand all the terms used in the question, and how should I interpret them?
- How *could* I respond to the question? What different approaches could I take?
- Which approach will allow me to address the learning outcomes, meet my tutor's expectations and present a strong argument in answer to the question?
- How will the word count affect the approach I choose?

Some examples

Consider the example assignment questions below. The three right-hand columns will depend on your assignment guidance, learning outcomes and marking criteria. But this table shows how you can begin to think about your task.

Assignment question	What is it really asking?	What is it inviting you to do?	Top tips
There is no convincing evidence for the existence of life outside our solar system. Discuss. [Physics]	*Is* there any convincing evidence for life outside our solar system?	Find out whether there *is* evidence. Develop criteria for 'convincing' evidence. Examine the evidence and argue whether or not it can be considered convincing.	Assignment titles that are not actually a question are often asking 'How true is this statement?' You'll explore reasons why it could be true and reasons why it might not be. The evidence might lead you to conclude one way or another.

Assignment question	What is it really asking?	What is it inviting you to do?	Top tips
Does social media drive or hinder language development? [Linguistics]	In what ways does social media drive language development? In what ways does it hinder it? According to your review of the evidence, which does it seem to do most?	Consider what might constitute 'language development'. Search for evidence of the impact of social media on language development. Present an argument as to whether it mainly drives, mainly hinders, or perhaps does both?	If an assignment is asking a direct question, make sure your essay answers it! Address the question in your introduction, ensure each paragraph helps you answer it, and reinforce your response in your conclusion.

Assignment question	What is it really asking?	What is it inviting you to do?	Top tips
How effective is current UK health, safety and welfare legislation in the construction industry? What are the priorities for change? *Illustrate your answer with examples.* [Construction Management]	What do you know about the legislation? How well does it work in theory and in practice?	Investigate the legislation and apply it to the construction industry. State clearly what you mean by 'effective'. Locate key problems and the realistic key priorities. Carefully select examples and use them to help you make your points.	Consider breaking the question into three parts: 1 Establish the context by consulting the literature. Consider legislation + role of HSE + inspection/size of site. 2 Define the word 'effectiveness'; that's crucial. 3 Who decides the priorities? Which ones are realistic in the current circumstances?

Remember: questions that ask you to use examples usually want to see those examples woven in throughout the assignment. Demonstrate how your arguments are reflected in real-life situations.

JUDGE

EVALUATE

Considering the learning outcomes and guidance

Your assignment may have a set of learning outcomes attached to it. These indicate what all students should have learned by the end of each module, and assignments are a way of demonstrating you've learned them. Although these outcomes are important, they can cause confusion. You have your main assignment question, but you also have this list of learning outcomes to address. It is tempting to just write about each outcome in turn, but this can result in a disjointed, list-like essay with no clear argument.

A better approach might be to:

- Look at the learning outcomes before you start planning and researching, and think about how they relate to your assignment question. Be aware that you will need to show understanding of them *in the course of answering the question*.
- Do your research and identify the argument you want to make. Focus on the points you want to present and plan a logical structure for your essay. *Keep the learning outcomes in mind but don't let them dictate the structure of your response*.
- Look again at the learning outcomes, and decide how best to address them *in the process of putting forward your argument*. Your understanding of them should emerge at relevant points. Once you have written your first draft, check that all the learning outcomes have been clearly met in the course of your argument.

Find out more about learning outcomes in *Planning Your Essay* in this series.

Considering the marking criteria

Before you start planning, researching or writing, you should know what's going to get you a high mark. Look carefully through all the assignment guidance and marking criteria. If you have been given a suggested structure, use it! If your tutors make recommendations, follow them!

Most mark schemes award credit for critical analysis. If you present a focused, well-evidenced argument (with the help of this book!), critical analysis will play an essential role. For more on critical reading and writing, see *Getting Critical* in this series.

Below is an example mark scheme for a history essay. It shows that the tutors are looking for a convincing, original argument, which uses evidence wisely and communicates ideas well. By 'original', tutors tend to mean that you are not just regurgitating ideas you've read or heard in a lecture, but are showing that you can think for yourself.

High-quality indicators	First	2:1	2:2	Third	Low-quality indicators
Demonstrates excellent knowledge, all relevant to the question	*Not just any knowledge!*				Barely any relevant knowledge or evidence of study
Demonstrates originality of interpretation and analysis	*Don't be afraid to offer an original perspective or interpretation, as long as you have evidence to support it.*				No attempt to interpret or analyse material used
Offers a convincing, clear argument in response to the question	*Convincing and clear!* *Note the word 'identifiable'. Your argument might be there somewhere, but if the reader can't identify it, they can't give you credit for it.*				Nothing identifiable as an argument in response to the question
Demonstrates skills in evaluation, analysis and synthesis of evidence in the writing	*Synthesis: bringing together different ideas or concepts to construct your own meaning.*				Little or no examples or evidence used to support ideas

Use your evidence wisely.

High-quality indicators	First	2:1	2:2	Third	Low-quality indicators
Uses academic conventions such as accurate referencing	*Be professional.*				Little or no use of recognised conventions for presenting academic work
Communicates ideas clearly and logically	*The way you write is important too – communicating your message.*				Ideas are hard to follow and frequent writing errors impede understanding

We'll show you how to communicate clearly.

Remember, an essay is a way of assessing that you:

▸ understand the subject you've been studying
▸ can apply what you've learned and what you've read
▸ can think beyond the content of lectures
▸ have read widely and can draw conclusions from the literature
▸ are capable of bringing together (synthesising) ideas to form a response to a specific question.

Getting started: initial ideas

Once you have analysed your question and the assessment criteria, it can be helpful to do some brainstorming, even before you begin to research. At this stage, keep an open mind; you can't decide on an argument until you've reviewed the evidence. However, it can be a good idea to consider your instinctive response to these questions:

▶ Can you give a one-sentence answer to your assignment question, based on what you already know?
▶ Can you expand that into three sentences explaining why you gave that answer?

Your response may change as you do further research, but focusing on the question in this way can get you into the 'argument' mindset from the start.

Summary

Think carefully about what your assignment is asking you to do. There may be different ways you could tackle it, and you should consider which approach is most appropriate, given the constraints of the question, word count and criteria.

Now that you've considered the expectations of your task, it's time to research and review evidence, in preparation for creating a well-informed argument. Part 2 will deal with finding information and gathering ideas.

PUTTING IDEAS TOGETHER

You have already thought about the task and have planned out a strategy including timescales. You now need to research your topic in order to generate ideas, gather evidence and eventually decide on your argument. Part 2 will show you how to go about this.

3 Finding out

Before going to library catalogues or search engines, it's a good idea to establish what you already know. We suggest you write down:

▶ what you know, e.g. from lecture notes and slides, material available in the school or department, guidance from tutors, etc.

▶ where the gaps are in your knowledge that need to be filled during your research.

It is helpful to put this into a form that you can gradually expand as you learn more about the topic. You will undoubtedly already have a system. But why not try experimenting with a new one? Techniques include:

▶ brainstorming
▶ pattern maps
▶ keywords
▶ knowledge maps
▶ tables
▶ pictures
▶ lists

Let's look at an example. Dan is undertaking an assignment on *the impact of COVID-19 on homelessness in the UK* for his Social Policy degree. Here is his first attempt to map out what he knows.

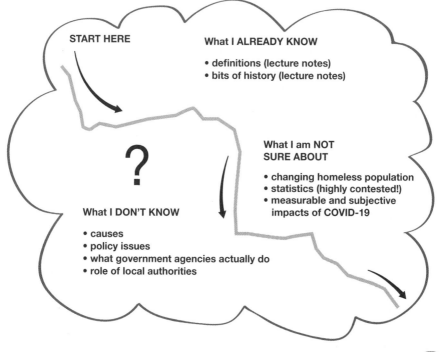

START HERE

What I ALREADY KNOW

• definitions (lecture notes)
• bits of history (lecture notes)

?

What I am NOT SURE ABOUT

• changing homeless population
• statistics (highly contested!)
• measurable and subjective impacts of COVID-19

What I DON'T KNOW

• causes
• policy issues
• what government agencies actually do
• role of local authorities

Establish what you need to find out

Establishing what you need to find out is a challenge, because you don't know what you don't know! You can't fill in all the gaps in one session. Normally, the questions become clarified and hopefully answered as you progress through your reading. Below are some key sources to search, discover and then use to fill in gaps in your knowledge.

Reading lists

Consult the reading list that relates to the assignment. Remember that you are not expected to read everything on the reading list. It's important guidance, but learn to be selective. As you begin to form your argument, you can focus on the literature that is most relevant to what you want to explore. There's more on reading lists in *Getting Critical* in this series.

Additional sources

In addition to the key items flagged up on your reading lists, your tutor may have suggested background material. You might also follow up further reading in books and journal articles. Evidence of further reading helps to distinguish between an average assignment and an outstanding one.

Key materials

The normal approach to finding information in the literature is to go from general to specific, as the figure below illustrates. You cannot form an argument unless you have a sound understanding of the key concepts. There are resources out there that can help you to understand the basics, including handbooks, encyclopedias and tools such as Wikipedia. However, don't reference Wikipedia directly in your assignment.

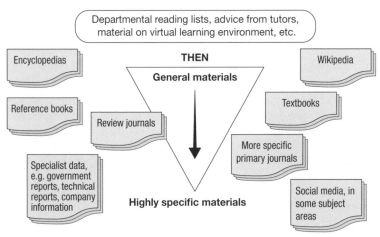

Consult your subject librarian

Your subject librarian is a key resource in your discipline. Subject librarians are experienced in the language of the discipline and may be able to recommend additional databases, ebooks and other resources to use. They can advise you on selecting and storing your information, and also referencing it.

For more information on searching, see *Where's Your Evidence?* in this series.

Finding out and moving forward

When you have begun to develop a plan, you will soon start to know more about:
- gaps in your knowledge
- the language of the discipline you are studying, including key terms
- important writers who have helped to shape the main concepts, theories and debates in the discipline.

What are the highly efficient means of actually reading these sources and compiling valuable notes?

Find out more in Chapter 4.

4   Developing your ideas

Effective reading skills will help you when gathering ideas. Always gain an overview of a document by looking at its structure. This is much more effective than starting at the beginning and working through paragraph by paragraph.

Reading actively: get an overview

How does the document you're reading fit together? It's easy to find out.

Scan for keywords

Try reading the document very quickly several times, to get a general 'feel' for the layout and the central points or keywords.

Skim the document for structure

Look out for headings and subheadings, and images and artwork. The diagram on the next page shows you how to do this.

1 Survey the text critically. Look at:

Title	Subtitle	Blurb	Author(s)	Date of publication	Contents (for overview) Index (for specifics)

2 Get an overview. Look for and skim:

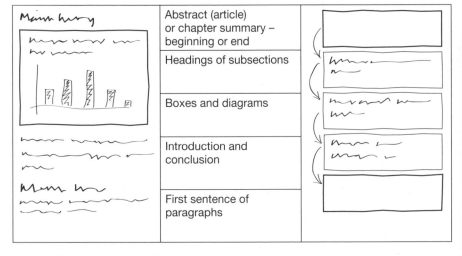

	Abstract (article) or chapter summary – beginning or end
	Headings of subsections
	Boxes and diagrams
	Introduction and conclusion
	First sentence of paragraphs

Source: Williams (2022) *Getting Critical*, with thanks.

Read purposefully

Read with a focus on what you want to find out, that is, read purposefully. Start with the abstract and the conclusion to identify the document's main ideas. Ruthlessly ignore anything that appears to be irrelevant.

Use technology

Use apps that incorporate annotation tools, or text-to-speech readers, to take some of the stress out of reading. Have a look at electronic note-making tools such as OneNote®, which can help you build ideas by bringing together class notes, references, sketches, photos and voice files.

Read actively

Ask yourself questions as you read the material. Let's return to Dan (BSc Social Policy), and his essay on how COVID-19 has impacted on homelessness.

> *The homelessness monitor: England 2021* ◄········ *Should I look at this report?*
>
> Suzanne Fitzpatrick, Beth Watts, Hal Pawson, Glen Bramley, Jenny Wood, Mark Stephens & Janice Blenkinsopp
>
> Institute for Social Policy, Housing and Equalities Research (I-SPHERE), Heriot-Watt University; City Futures Research Centre, University of New South Wales; School of Social and Political Sciences, University of Glasgow ◄
>
> *Quality of authors and institutions?*
>
> For Crisis
> March 2021 ◄········ *Is the report up-to-date?*

Have your own glossary by your side, which you can constantly update with new or unusual technical words.

> *Have you started keeping a list of technical terms in your discipline? If not, start a glossary today!*

For more on reading techniques, see *Reading and Making Notes* in this series.

Active note-making

At the note-making stage, you are forming an initial response to what you are reading. This should be an active process. You are not just writing something down, you have to think about it, consider its link to your assignment question and to other things you've read. Additionally, you need to reflect on how to make use of its information. Note-making also means actively rejecting material that might be interesting but irrelevant.

Tips for active note-making

Do	Don't
Be ruthless! Only read material that is essential to the task.	Get side-tracked by reading material that is interesting but irrelevant.
Note key points.	Simply write out long sentences – comforting but not helpful.
Make sure quotes are clearly identified.	Mix up specific quotations with your own thoughts and ideas – that way lies problems with plagiarism!
Make links between different parts of the text, or between the text and your own ideas, in order to customise it and make sense of it.	Highlight sentences and think that you are 'taking notes' – you are not!

Do	Don't
Keep using your notes! Integrate them into a knowledge map for the assignment, so that the ideas relate to what you already know.	Put your notes in a folder, leave them on a shelf and then forget about them.

Managing your information

At an early stage, decide how you're going to:

▶ record your information

▶ store it, e.g. in A4 files, a database, spreadsheet, bibliography or research notebook

▶ learn how to cite what you found using reference management tools, free apps like Mendeley, or browser extensions such as Zotero.

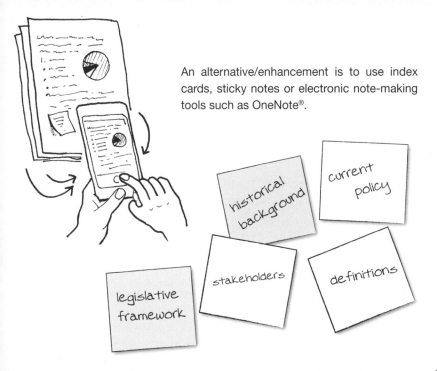

An alternative/enhancement is to use index cards, sticky notes or electronic note-making tools such as OneNote®.

historical background

current policy

stakeholders

definitions

legislative framework

Evaluating the material and critical questions

As you go through your notes, it helps to be constantly evaluating, asking yourself: 'Do I need this? Will it help me?' A great technique is to use questions that stimulate critical thinking. You might want to make these questions into a one-page A4 template, or simply keep them by you as you walk through the evidence.

Examples of critical questions:
▸ **Who** is the author of this material?
▸ **Where** are they based?
▸ **What** is the point of this material?
▸ **What** do I want to take from this material?
▸ **How** do I want to use it?

For more information on questions to help critical thinking, see *Getting Critical* and *Time Management* in this series.

You have now targeted the helpful information, read it, made notes and begun to develop your ideas. The next stage is shaping those ideas into evidence and then into a consistent and compelling argument.

5 Evidence

Tutors often use the word 'evidence' to mean two things:

1 They are looking for an indication that you have understood the topic and are thinking about it critically. So, a lecturer might want to see **evidence of your understanding**. We will show you how to demonstrate your understanding in Parts 3 and 4.

2 They also use the word **evidence** in a general academic sense; anything that backs up and supports a statement or claim that you make. However, the word 'evidence' is rather slippery.

Different kinds of evidence in different disciplines

This chapter is about collecting and assembling evidence. This will vary between disciplines. For instance, philosophers and food safety experts will have different perspectives on what constitutes evidence.

You may encounter two major approaches to research, generally known as 'quantitative' or 'qualitative' methods.

Type of data	Sometimes known as	What does that mean?	Examples
Quantitative	'Hard data'	Numeric data; numbers that can be measured.	Results from a laboratory experiment. Numbers from a survey.
Qualitative	'Soft data'	Qualities that can't easily be measured.	Conversations with hospital patients. Emotional reactions to advertising.

There are also different standards of interpretation of data, depending on the discipline. For instance, civil engineers might have different standards of statistical interpretation of data from social workers or teachers. The way you use the evidence you have collected is very much connected with the particular schools of thought and research methods common in your discipline. However, you may well have to work with both qualitative and quantitative data during your degree. As always, be guided by your tutors.

Evaluating evidence as you build your argument

Because some evidence is more relevant and useful than others, it is always helpful to **evaluate** your evidence carefully. To help you choose your evidence, you need some simple tools. There is a real skill in questioning the evidence and then questioning your own responses to the evidence.

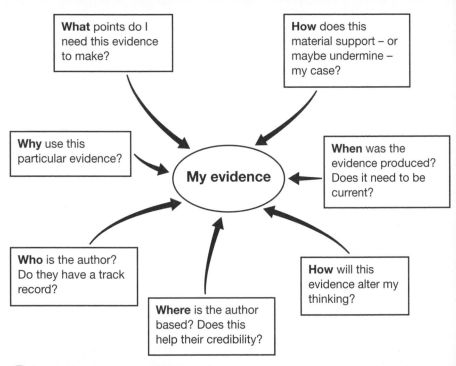

What points do I need this evidence to make?

How does this material support – or maybe undermine – my case?

Why use this particular evidence?

My evidence

When was the evidence produced? Does it need to be current?

Who is the author? Do they have a track record?

Where is the author based? Does this help their credibility?

How will this evidence alter my thinking?

Your use of evidence **should**:

▶ **indicate** what other scholars have written or said about your topic
▶ **show** how new ideas impact on your thinking
▶ **integrate** with your ideas
▶ help to **form** and **support** your argument
▶ **illustrate** key points
▶ **develop** the complexity of your argument (partly through considering counterarguments)
▶ **change** and **redirect** the argument when necessary.

Your use of evidence **should not**:

▶ give the impression that references are being used just for show
▶ undermine or confuse your argument
▶ be manipulated to support your opinion, ignoring other equally valid views.

What kinds of evidence?

The evidence you collect normally comes from either **primary** or **secondary** sources. The mix of primary and secondary sources you use will depend on your discipline, the question you're answering and the approach of your tutors.

	Specific type of material	Data
Primary sources	Experiments, observations, interviews and specific documents on a subject, e.g. research studies, maps, poems, objects, blogs. Original collections, e.g. statistics, diaries and so on.	Either your own data, e.g., from observation, or data collected by others.
Secondary sources	Journal articles, books, conference papers, analysis of statistics or data and websites.	Other people's analysis and interpretation of data.

Characteristics of evidence

Evidence has to be:

Primary sources

- **Valid:** Does it measure what it sets out to measure?
- **Reliable:** Is the evidence accurate and consistent?
- **Credible:** Is it believable? Credibility depends on a range of factors, such as those shown below.

Secondary sources

Factors affecting the credibility of your evidence

Factor	Comment
The authority of the publication in which the evidence appeared.	Just because evidence is published in a journal or on a website does not necessarily make it accurate.
The background and authority of the author.	Much depends on the subject discipline. In a scientific subject, the author would be expected to be employed in a reputable scientific institution. The author would normally be expected to have produced previous papers.
The approach of the author (important in most disciplines).	So far as you can tell, has the author declared their theoretical approach? Is there an obvious bias or interpretation that has not been declared?
The currency of the source. Is the material up to date?	The importance of the date of the evidence will vary across disciplines. In some subjects such as art history, an older document is highly relevant when it demonstrates how critics thought at that time. In other subjects, e.g. in the sciences, you are expected to be aware of current research, which builds on previous studies.
If data are involved, how were the data collected?	Has the researcher clearly stated the methods they used?

Selecting evidence: an example

Let's look at Dan's assignment on how COVID-19 has impacted on homelessness. He's been collecting materials and deciding what to include in his assignment. The table below shows how he is selecting evidence.

Source material on homelessness	Should I select?
Item 1 (Report) Fitzpatrick, S. et al. (2021) *The homelessness monitor: England 2021.* Crisis: London. Online. Available at: www.crisis.org.uk/media/244702/crisis-england-monitor-2021.pdf	*Yes!* *Reasonably current. Loads of relevant stats, e.g. page 45. Useful bibliography* *Essential*
Item 2 (Briefing paper) UK Parliament. House of Commons Library (2021) *Coronavirus: support for rough sleepers (England).* Research briefing. Online. Available at: https://commonslibrary.parliament.uk/research-briefings/cbp-9057/	*Yes!* *Absolute GOLD on legislation! Plus references! (Note to self – ask subject librarian exactly how to reference this)*

Source material on homelessness	Should I select?
Item 3 (Policy document) Department for Levelling Up, Housing and Communities (2018) *Homelessness code of guidance for local authorities.* Online. Available as PDF at: www.gov.uk/guidance/homelessness-code-of-guidance-for-local-authorities	*Yes.* *I suppose. Pre-Covid, but helpful in setting out the statutory duties of local authorities, but only IN ENGLAND! What was supposed to happen pre-Covid? Excellent background. Check my essay title? Can critique in my assignment?*
Item 4 (Blog) Watts, B. (2021) Reducing rough sleeping: lessons from Greater Manchester's A Bed Every Night programme. Online. Available at: www.i-sphere.hw.ac.uk/reducing-rough-sleeping-lessons-from-greater-manchesters-a-bed-every-night-programme/	**No.** *I won't use this. It's a blog, based on ongoing research. Looks really interesting BUT maybe I should rely on research that has already been published and peer-reviewed? Follow up this author, though!*

Evidence in theory and in practice

Many courses, and almost all professional ones, will include assignments that challenge students to combine the published literature (theory) with their own observations, reflections or experiences (practice). These practical experiences, such as work placements or case studies, also provide forms of evidence, which complement what you find in the literature. The skill here is to show how what you have discovered in practice relates to theoretical models and arguments. We develop this idea further in Chapter 13.

Conflicting evidence

Your role as a scholar is to evaluate and bring together different perspectives on the topic. It's worth remembering that 'evidence' can be a slippery concept. It is sometimes contested – experts disagree – and sometimes different kinds of evidence are set up against each other. One of your jobs in an assignment will be to present and evaluate different viewpoints, which means examining evidence from different perspectives.

This is what a 'nuanced' argument is all about! To illustrate, here's a dialogue between a lecturer and a student studying social policy:

Student: 'I want to argue that the key factor that predicts mental ill-health is social inequality. So, for example, arguing for "better mental health services" is not sufficient.'

Lecturer: 'Okay – why do you think that?'

Student: 'Because so much evidence now points to our social circumstances being the key factor in our mental health.'

Lecturer: 'Right, mental health isn't linked to physical health, physical health isn't a key factor, is that what you're saying?'

Student: 'No, but it is complex. Physical health is important but so are all aspects of social inequality, including income.'

Lecturer: 'So show me how you make sense of the evidence when you write your assignment.'

As you collect evidence, here are four key considerations:

Do	Potential trap	Comment
1 **Explain why evidence is important.**	Avoid using freestanding evidence without explanation.	Evidence needs a context to support it. See more in Chapter 12.
2 **Select evidence with care.**	Do not attempt to shovel in all the evidence you can find.	Quality counts.
3 **Ensure that each piece of evidence clearly contributes to an argument.**	Avoid filling your pages with vague 'evidence', and then losing sight of your theme.	Everything you select should have a function in supporting your argument.
4 **Keep checking your evidence against your thesis statement or hypothesis.**	Don't think rigidly; reconsider your argument in the light of new evidence.	Keep summarising your main argument in one sentence to keep you on track.

Most of the time, finding your evidence should be relatively straightforward. The challenge is to think critically about it, select the appropriate material and find ways to demonstrate your judgements about the debate. For more on choosing your evidence and dealing with conflicting evidence, see *Where's Your Evidence?* in this series.

6 Forming an argument

The word 'argument' has several meanings. A tutor may use it to mean:

▶ **making a series of claims**, supported by evidence
▶ **constructing a case** in a logical way
▶ **presenting a point of view**.

As mentioned in the Introduction, tutors will usually expect you to construct an argument or make a case, even if the word 'argument' is not actually used in the assignment question.

An argument from your research

One of the skills of constructing your argument is to move through these stages.

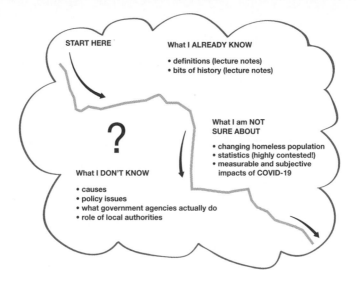

START HERE

What I ALREADY KNOW

• definitions (lecture notes)
• bits of history (lecture notes)

?

What I am NOT SURE ABOUT

• changing homeless population
• statistics (highly contested!)
• measurable and subjective impacts of COVID-19

What I DON'T KNOW

• causes
• policy issues
• what government agencies actually do
• role of local authorities

Let's look at the first part of the process.

Make an initial picture of your argument

When you are drafting your argument during the research and planning stage, it's easy to get confused. This is because our brain works in three dimensions, constantly receiving information that it translates into images, words and sounds. If we are fortunate, we experience all of our senses all the time. But when we write, we have to transform three-dimensional senses and thoughts into words, then sentences, in linear blocks.

We strongly recommend a (**visual planning stage**) between note-taking and writing.

Finding out
Reading and note-taking
Evidence
Forming your argument
Writing

So, how can we translate the whirling ideas in our brains into a rational and logical argument? Here is an effective tool for pinning down and exploring complicated ideas.

Step 1: Mind map

A mind map is a helpful way of capturing ideas about a topic. It is usually based on a central concept in the middle of the page, with subconcepts radiating out and arrows indicating links.

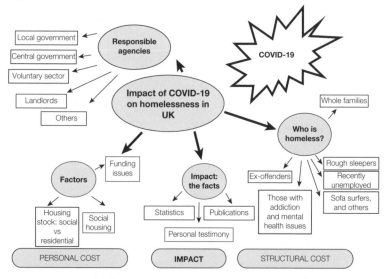

- **Upside:** It is intended to be quick and spontaneous.
- **Downside:** It is not intended to offer a logical framework for your ideas. This will come later.

Step 2: Picture your argument with a concept map

A concept map is a visual outline that shows the **relationships** between ideas.

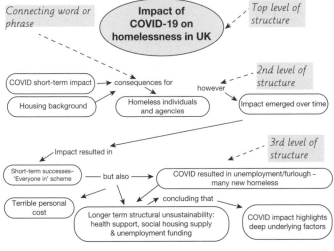

A concept map is more helpful than a mind map when you are thinking about logical relationships:

1 You have to order ideas in a series of **levels** or **hierarchies**.
2 You need **connections** to show how one concept links to another. These are indicated by short phrases, which help you to see logical relationships between ideas.

Just as important, the map helps you to cut out relationships that do not logically follow on one from another.

You can see examples of concept maps on the web, e.g. YouTube or SlideShare.com.

Step 3: Keep in mind a take-home message

As you begin to put your evidence together, it's important to focus on how you are responding to the learning outcomes and the question. To help you respond, we like the concept of the **take-home message**. What key point from your argument do you want to leave with the marker? For instance, with Dan's essay on homelessness and COVID-19, his take-home message might be:

---

1 **The causes of homelessness are highly complex.**
2 **The impact of the pandemic made a bad situation much worse.**
3 **Solutions always involve collaborations between government and nongovernmental agencies, especially in times of crisis.**

Your assignment must have a central focus. This might be there from the beginning of your preparation, or it might emerge slowly as you go through the planning and development phase.

There is more about structuring and sequencing your argument in Part 3. But think about your potential take-home message **before** you focus in much detail on your structure.

How to develop your argument

Here are some tips on making sure that your argument is well developed and logical:

- Even if you feel strongly about the topic, e.g., climate change, keep your argument evidence-based.
- Clearly define your terms.
- Acknowledge that there may sometimes be more than one point of view. Your job is to examine a range of viewpoints and then present your own case. As the Introduction to this book pointed out, your argument should contain complexity and nuance.

Constructing an argument is similar to arguing a case in a court trial: presenting a series of reasoned ideas, with evidence to back up each one, all of them joining up to convince the audience of a particular perspective.

Summary: putting ideas together

By searching for information, by active reading and note-taking, you will establish what you know, and begin to fill in the gaps in your knowledge. You can then start to build an argument, supporting it with valid evidence, to make a logical case. However, argument is not just about logic and evidence. It's also about **effectively conveying** your argument and that's what we turn to in Part 3.

At this stage, you will have:

▶ Considered your assignment question and how to approach your task.

▶ Done your research.

▶ Used that research to begin forming your own ideas in response to your assignment question, perhaps using mind maps or concept maps.

▶ Decided what you want to *say* – your central argument and 'take-home' message.

Now you need to:

▶ Decide on a series of points that will help the reader to understand and be convinced by your argument.

▶ Consider how to present the evidence that supports each of those points.

▶ Decide on the best structure for your points, so the reader can easily follow what you are saying.

Finding the best structure for all your ideas can be tricky. Here are some practical strategies to try:

▶ Write **each point** (probably selected from your initial mind map or concept map) on a separate index card and shuffle them around to find a logical flow. Imagine how you would make links from one point to the next.

▶ Alternatively, enter each point into a separate slide in Microsoft PowerPoint (or whatever presentation software you use), then drag and drop the slides to reorder them. This then becomes a plan for your essay, each slide representing a paragraph. You could play the slideshow to watch your line of reasoning rolling past.

▶ Try using **subheadings** to organise your ideas, even if you plan to remove them later (your department *may* discourage their use). By thinking about what subheadings you would use, and what would appear under them, you can start organising your ideas into themes.

One way of structuring an essay

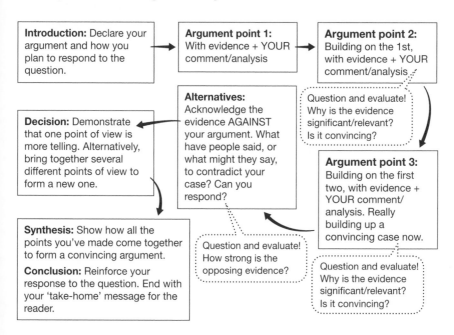

Introduction: Declare your argument and how you plan to respond to the question.

Argument point 1: With evidence + YOUR comment/analysis

Argument point 2: Building on the 1st, with evidence + YOUR comment/analysis

Question and evaluate! Why is the evidence significant/relevant? Is it convincing?

Argument point 3: Building on the first two, with evidence + YOUR comment/analysis. Really building up a convincing case now.

Question and evaluate! Why is the evidence significant/relevant? Is it convincing?

Alternatives: Acknowledge the evidence AGAINST your argument. What have people said, or what might they say, to contradict your case? Can you respond?

Question and evaluate! How strong is the opposing evidence?

Decision: Demonstrate that one point of view is more telling. Alternatively, bring together several different points of view to form a new one.

Synthesis: Show how all the points you've made come together to form a convincing argument.

Conclusion: Reinforce your response to the question. End with your 'take-home' message for the reader.

Remember: the structure above contains the building blocks of an argument, but assignments can vary enormously. Consult your assignment guidance to see what else you need to incorporate along the way, such as addressing specific learning outcomes or including real-life examples. Consider where and how you can incorporate the requirements of your task, while still maintaining a clear and solid structure for your argument.

An example: Yuyan's essay plan

Yuyan is a first-year student working on a 1,500 word essay for her sociolinguistics module:

Does social media drive or hinder language development?

She has done her research, reviewed the evidence and ideas of other scholars and decided on the position she wants to argue. Yuyan's overall argument is:

Social media drives language development in the sense that it allows large numbers of people to contribute to the rapid evolution of a language.

The points Yuyan wants to make

Yuyan wants to make the following points, generated by a concept map, based on her research:

New words being created all the time – selfie, googled, friended, vlog, smartphone, livestream (evidence from OED). Everyone has potential to influence language (McKean, 2002). Shakespeare introduced new words into the Eng lang – social media doing same?

Different registers and forms of language becoming more relevant/widespread. Social media changes 'linguistic and communicative practices' (Seargeant and Tagg, 2014).

Meanings of existing words also changing – troll, surfing, cloud, tweeting.

Online conversations encourage skills of debating, collaborating, creating shared discussion/story (Lunenfeld, 2011).

Does social media encourage 'textspeak'? Only a negative thing if you consider Standard English the most prestigious form (Crystal and Sledd's ideas about Standard English).

How to define 'language development'? If it just means becoming skilled at Standard English in traditional sense, maybe social media isn't helpful. If 'language development' means the evolution of language, social media drives it on a large scale. (NB: models of 'language change' slightly different to, but related to, models of 'language development'.)

Putting these points into a structure

Before she can decide where to start, Yuyan needs to think again about where she is heading. She reminds herself of her intended conclusion, and then considers how to order her points so they will build effectively towards it.

▶ She realises that her argument promotes a wider view of 'language' than just grammatical rules and standards. Therefore, she decides to start by addressing the viewpoint she wants to challenge.

▶ Now she finds it easier to build the steps in between. As she forms her plan, she keeps asking herself: Where would be a logical place to go from here? What is the connection between this step of my argument and the next? How do I carry my reader from my starting point to my conclusion, so that by the time we get there, they'll be convinced? At this stage, she might spot some weaknesses in her argument, and may need to gather further evidence. She also considers how many words she has available to make each point.

▶ Yuyan puts her key ideas onto sticky notes, then moves them into a logical sequence before sticking them to a large piece of paper. She notes the links between each of her points, so she can see how her argument will flow.

Here is her plan:

The popular press (give examples) discusses the idea that social media encourages 'textspeak' and non-standard grammar. However, this is only negative if you consider Standard English the most prestigious form of our language (Crystal, 2007). Different registers and forms of language are becoming more relevant/widespread (sociolinguistic perspective).

LINK: Use of Standard English is not the only way of looking at 'language development' ... also about discourse and interaction

Online conversations encourage the skill of debating, collaborating, creating a shared discussion/story (Lunenfeld, 2011).

LINK: Collaboration leads to the evolution of language, e.g. creation of new words

New words being created – selfie, googled, friended, vlog, smartphone, livestream (OED). Anybody has the potential to influence language (McKean, 2002; Seargeant and Tagg, 2014; Jones et al., 2021). Meanings of existing words also changing – troll, surfing, tweeting, cloud.

LINK: New words reflect our changing society. Society is not static; neither is language

How do we define 'language development'? If it just means refining English skills in the traditional sense, perhaps social media is not helpful. But if it means the evolution of language, social media drives it on a large scale (bring back to Crystal's ideas).

CONCLUDE: The suggestion that social media encourages poor language skills stems from a narrow view of 'language development'. Social media drives language development in the sense that it allows large amounts of people to contribute to the rapid evolution of language

The structure may change as Yuyan writes and redrafts, but she will begin with a clear idea of her argument, the points she wants to make and the evidence that supports those points. This will help her create a focused, progressive response.

You might notice that Yuyan has planned her conclusion but not her introduction. It is much easier to write your introduction once you've written the rest of your essay. Find out more about introductions and conclusions in Chapter 10.

Chapter 8 will focus on the structure of paragraphs within your assignment.

Imagine your essay as a flight of stairs, down which you smoothly guide your reader, towards your conclusion. They can see where they're going and feel secure that you're leading them. Each of your paragraphs is a step towards that destination, joined to the step before and the step after.

However, each paragraph is a miniature staircase too! This chapter will show you how to manage and structure your paragraphs so they contribute effectively to your argument.

Make each section of your argument pull its weight!

Each paragraph or section should:

- **Progress** your argument, making just **one** clear point in support of it.
- Present a **reason** why the reader should be convinced by your argument. Even if you are

acknowledging counterarguments, this helps the reader to trust you as it shows you are thorough. This will help your case when you then discredit or challenge them.

▶ Present clear **evidence** to support each reason.

Within each paragraph, there may be some material that is there merely to reinforce things, link back to points previously made, or help the reader navigate through the argument. But most of your words should be dedicated to the progression of your argument.

Paragraph structure

You can often think of paragraphs as miniature essays, discussing, supporting and criticising a **single idea**. Their structure may vary depending on your essay question and subject, and complex points may stretch across two or three paragraphs, but below is an example template. Other Pocket Guides in this series offer slightly different, but complementary, templates, so use the one that most appeals to you. They all work on a similar principle about the elements of a good paragraph.

1 **Introduce your point:** The first sentence should show the reader what the paragraph is going to discuss. Keep these sentences concise and clear. The reader needs to be able to follow your argument clearly.

2 **Elaborate on the point you have introduced:** Having introduced it in a clear and snappy way, you can now explain further, helping the reader to fully understand this step in your argument.

3 **Provide evidence:** Summarise and reference the evidence that supports the point you are making.

4 **Comment on the evidence:** Criticise, interpret or engage with the evidence you've introduced. What does it demonstrate? How does it support your point? What do YOU want to say about this evidence and the point you've made in this paragraph?

5 **Conclude your point:** Summarise the point you've made, and indicate what it means for your overall argument. This is your '**so what?**' sentence. You have presented the reader with information, evidence and analysis – but they should not be left wondering 'so what?' Emphasise the contribution this paragraph has made to your overall argument.

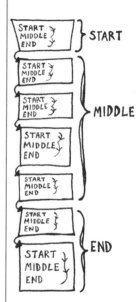

A paragraph example

Below is a paragraph from Yuyan's essay 'Does social media drive or hinder language development?', cited in Chapter 7. Consider the structure of the paragraph and the way she links her point to her main argument. Much of her paragraph is dedicated to analysis and discussion, rather than just description.

Although grammar and Standard English are grounded in quite rigid rules, language in the broader sense is constantly evolving, and social media plays a significant role. Many recent additions or changes to the Oxford Dictionary Online have emerged from social media, such as livestream (2021), smartphone (2014), selfie (2013), vlog (2009) and hashtag (2009). Although many of these new words are controversial, they reflect our changing society. They show a modern emphasis on brevity (abbreviations such as selfie), and also shared, public conversation, with 'hashtag' indicating a

This is the point Yuyan intends to make in this paragraph.

Here she has included some examples to help illustrate and evidence her point.

She goes on to discuss these examples and what they show us about language development – this is her voice and her analysis coming through.

trend for applying tags to conversational themes that can be searched for and contributed to by millions worldwide. The word 'tweet' is a particularly interesting example. It was officially added to the Oxford English Dictionary in its social media sense in 2013, bypassing their requirement that words and meanings have to be in usage for at least ten years before they can enter the dictionary. Their justification was the fiftyfold increase in usage of the word 'tweet' from 2006 to 2012 (Oxford Dictionaries, 2013). This suggests that social media is not only driving language development; it is doing so at a rapid rate, perhaps because of the instantaneous, collaborative and global nature of modern communication.

Her final sentence has a clear link into her main argument. Phrases like 'This suggests' help indicate the relevance of the ideas to the reader. She also uses some of the words from the question – 'driving language development' – to make it explicit that this paragraph has contributed something towards answering it.

Try applying this checklist to ensure that each paragraph is doing its job:

▶ Is your first sentence a clear, concise indication of the point you want to make in this paragraph?

▶ Does the rest of the paragraph build on that first sentence, or have you drifted away?

▶ Do the first and last sentences of the paragraph relate to each other and to your overall argument?

▶ Have you included evidence, and explained its relevance?

▶ Is there enough analysis/discussion? If the paragraph is mostly a paraphrase of another source, or crowded with quotes, perhaps there is not enough commentary.

▶ Does this paragraph help you to answer the question, and will your reader be able to see how it does so?

▶ Is the paragraph long enough to show your reader that your point has been properly developed, but short enough that its central focus remains sharp?

What about counterarguments?

In order to convince your reader, you need to show that you have examined your assignment question from more than one perspective and acknowledged arguments that disagree with your principal ones. Using the tools in this book, you will be able to demonstrate that you're aware of other perspectives, but that the evidence which supports *your* case is more convincing – which is why you are arguing it in the first place! However, you don't have to deal with every stray argument that disagrees with your own. Work with strong, relevant counterarguments and impress your tutor by critiquing them.

Chapter 12 offers further advice on how to acknowledge different points of view.

Once you have a structure in place, you should be able to write much more easily than if you had leapt straight from reading to writing. Let go of perfectionism when you write your first draft. Expand your structure into an essay and get your ideas in place, no matter how rough your writing might be at this stage. When you start redrafting, you then need to think about the flow and clarity of your argument. 'Flow' turns your piece of writing from a string of disjointed paragraphs into a journey of connected ideas.

Using signposts

Achieving 'flow' begins with planning a logical structure, but you also need to guide the reader along that structure. **Signposts** are words and phrases that move the reader through your argument, and help it to make sense and feel progressive.

Use signposts:

▶ in your introduction to show the reader what to expect and indicate what you are going to argue

- at the start of each paragraph to show the point to be made
- at the end of each paragraph to remind readers of the link to the question, and to nudge them towards the next point
- within paragraphs – use words like 'however' and 'therefore' to make links between sentences.

Examples of signposts

Signpost	Where in the essay?	How does it help the reader?
This essay will argue, at a management-relevant scale, that human activities have a severe impact on coral reefs.	Introduction.	Indicates how you have chosen to approach the question. Tells the reader where you are heading, which makes your argument easier to follow from the start.
This is, however, a simplistic way of looking at the concept of patient-centred care.	At the start of a paragraph, explicitly linking to the previous paragraph.	Moves the argument on by directly challenging the idea that has come before. The pronoun 'this' makes a link with the previous paragraph. Be sure to only use pronouns (e.g. 'it', 'this', 'they') when it's clear what they refer to.
In order to examine this topic further, it is helpful to apply a sociolinguistic perspective.	At the start of a paragraph or section that will focus on a sociolinguistic perspective.	Warns the reader that a particular theory will now be applied – rather than leaping straight into the theory, which may leave them scrabbling to catch up.

Signpost	Where in the essay?	How does it help the reader?
This theory of transference and countertransference in psychotherapy can be seen in practice in Case Study B.	At the start of a paragraph, linking the theory in the previous paragraph to a real-life example to be discussed in this paragraph.	If your assignment requires you to compare or connect theory and practice, clearly show that you are doing this with signposts that make an explicit link between the two.
Small-scale signposts: ▸ *However* ▸ *Furthermore* ▸ *Consequently* ▸ *Therefore* ▸ *This shows* ▸ *Alternatively* ▸ *For example*	Throughout the essay.	Help navigate from idea to idea, sentence to sentence. Use them carefully, and in the right context! Only use 'however' if you really are challenging or amending a previous point. Only use 'consequently' if the idea that follows really is a consequence of the previous one.

Signposts in action

Let's have a look at a paragraph from an essay that Olivia (MSc Environmental Science) is writing on coral reef destruction. She has used signposts to guide the reader through. (NB: the references used here are fictional examples.)

Coral reefs have been observed recovering from natural disturbance (Nystrom et al., 2012), but their ability to do so is affected by human activities, many of which have not been fully investigated. Fishing is well studied and has been found to affect coral cover (Appleby et al., 2010; Mumford and Simpson, 2011). However, fishing is just one of many threats to reefs. Coastal development, pollution and damage by ships also have unknown levels of impact (Wilfred, 2011). The small number of reefs studied and even smaller number monitored longitudinally means that we know little about the extent of most of the greatest threats. In addition, understanding of social context, such as the dependence of local people on reef resources, is needed to ensure effective management of human activities affecting reefs.

Signposting the main point/theme of the paragraph.

Prepares the reader for what is to come: a list of other threats to reefs.

Small-scale signpost indicating the relationship between the ideas discussed so far, and the ones to come.

Ties in with the first sentence of the paragraph. The theme is consistent throughout, but there is also a sense of progression from the first sentence to the last.

Linking the ideas within the paragraph.

The paragraph is now set up to feed into the next one, which will further explore the 'social context' raised in that final sentence.

You will notice from the examples that each paragraph usually has a miniature introduction and conclusion. It is likely that you will make several intermediate conclusions throughout your essay, which will support your main one and help keep the reader focused on your argument. Chapter 10 provides some tips for writing your overall introduction and conclusion.

10 Beginnings and endings

In order to be well structured and professional, essays also need good quality introductions and conclusions. This chapter will offer advice for starting and ending strongly.

Your conclusion

At the end of your essay, you will need to:

- Synthesise (bring together) the key points of your essay.
- Remind the reader of your overall argument, and how your key points have supported it.
- Reinforce your answer to the question – one final chance to make it completely clear that you've answered it, and met the learning outcomes along the way!
- Leave the reader with a 'take-home' message.

You may wish to:

- Highlight any implications that your argument has for the wider field.
- Recommend areas for future research.

Tips for conclusions

▶ No new information should be introduced that hasn't been discussed in the main body of your assignment. Your reader should feel satisfied and convinced by your argument, rather than surprised or confused by a whole new direction.

▶ Be as specific as possible. Avoid generic conclusions that could be tagged on to the end of any essay. This is your chance to leave the reader with a clear picture of the unique argument you've presented. There should be a sense that your essay has achieved what it set out to achieve.

Example conclusion

Below is the concluding paragraph from Simon (BSc Physiotherapy) for an essay entitled:

Does the study of proprioception have a significant impact on rehabilitation?

In conclusion, there is substantial evidence to suggest that studying proprioception does have a significant positive impact on rehabilitation. It has been shown to

Direct link to question.

improve functional outcome and reduce length of stay in hospital, in both musculoskeletal and neurological rehabilitation programmes. However, as this essay has indicated, there is also a small amount of contradictory evidence, suggesting that proprioception awareness may not always have a significant effect during rehabilitation. Therefore, rehabilitation programmes should not be completely oriented around proprioception. Instead, they should be combined with other rehabilitation processes to ensure that patients have the best chance of recovery.

Specific key points summarised.

Highlighting the arguments that have been made.

The 'take-home' message of the essay.

Your introduction

This is the final part of this chapter because your introduction is the final thing you should write! Once you've completed the main body and conclusion, you'll be in a better position to write a focused, concise introduction that tells the reader what to expect from the rest of the essay.

It's the last thing you'll write, but the first thing your tutor will read. They'll be looking for a clear idea of how you have approached the question. Your assignment will probably have been submitted anonymously, so they won't know who has written it, or whether you are a conscientious student likely to have built a strong argument based on rigorous research. It's up to you to demonstrate this, starting with a strong introduction to set the tone.

Your introduction should contain:

- Direct reference to the question, and, if appropriate, short definitions of key terms.
- Any **brief** background information the reader might need in order to glide easily into your argument. Avoid padding it with general waffle. Writing your introduction last will help you resist this temptation, as you will have included the necessary background information at relevant points throughout the main body of your essay, so you shouldn't feel the need to cram it all in at the start.
- A clear statement of what you intend to argue in your essay.
- A specific outline of what will be discussed. Again, this is much easier to write once you have written the rest of the assignment!

You may also wish to:

- Justify why you have chosen to focus on certain aspects of a topic.
- Quantify your aims or the content of your essay ('This essay will discuss **three** approaches to …').

Example introduction

Below is the introduction to Armand's BSc Political Science essay entitled:

Explain the main differences between Classical Realism and Neorealism. Which approach offers the best tools for analysing current international affairs?

This essay will argue that Neorealism is a more useful tool for understanding current affairs than Classical Realism. In order to make this argument, the essay will first outline the differences between Classical Realism and Neorealism, with reference to their perspectives on human nature and the role of international actors and structures. It will then present a series of examples in current affairs, to demonstrate the comparative advantages and disadvantages of using the theories to make sense of these events. Finally, the essay will discuss the preference for Neorealism, with reference to why international structures are essential to understanding international affairs, and therefore why Neorealism is a more useful tool.

This writer has stated their argument immediately.

Very specific signposting of what is to come. Indicates exactly how the question will be answered (without just repeating the question).

It is unlikely that this student could have written such a clear, to-the-point introduction before writing the rest of their essay and their conclusion. Chances are they would have waffled their way into their argument, or ended up with an introduction and main body that did not match.

Summary: building your argument

A logical structure is essential to a convincing argument. Structure and signposting allow your reader to move through your line of reasoning, and you must help them in any way you can.

Part 4 will explore another key tool for communicating your argument: presenting evidence effectively.

SHOWING YOUR ARGUMENT

To be a scholar, whatever your discipline, you need to learn how to:

) **present evidence** (Chapter 11)
) **communicate with your reader** (Chapter 12)
) **develop your academic voice** (Chapter 13).

These chapters will help you to learn more about communicating an evidence-based argument.

How you use evidence will depend on the conventions in your discipline. Your experience of evidence may vary, depending, for instance, on whether you are writing up a lab-based experiment, studying transcripts of interviews with social work clients, or reflecting on work-based or placement learning. The way you analyse and present your evidence will depend on the way in which your discipline undertakes research. This has an impact on **what** you present and **how** you present it. For example, it will affect the way you:

▶ use your citations in the text

▶ quote in the text

▶ use footnotes.

Interrogating your evidence

A golden rule for the use of evidence in any discipline is to question it. Ask yourself critical questions, such as:

- What exactly is the evidence?
- What methods were used?
- What might this evidence mean?
- Why are the results like this?
- How does this evidence fit into my argument?
- Should it make me change my thinking?
- Have I got enough evidence now?
- How do I avoid overwhelming my reader with evidence?
- When do I stop collecting and start writing?

Some ways of using evidence

In many disciplines, a large part of your evidence will be literature based, such as ideas and quotations. The example on the next page shows some of the skills you can demonstrate through your use of evidence.

Demonstrate your grasp of the conventions.

Show you understand the literature.

Question evidence and demonstrate your own critical thinking.

It has long been recognised that clinicians benefit from using medical evidence to support their practice. In 1992, however, the formation of the Evidence-Based Medicine Working Group, at McMaster University in Canada, saw the launch of a new paradigm of medical decision-making, 'evidence-based medicine'. Since then, there has been a growing emphasis in the literature on promoting clinical decisions made on the basis of best current evidence.

In its *Information for Health: An information strategy* for *the modern NHS 1998–2005* (NHSE, 1998), the NHS made a commitment to training its staff in the effective use of information. As well as acknowledging the need for staff to have access to sources of evidence, it stressed that they need the skills to be able to 'use evidence to inform practice'. It also acknowledged, however, the obstacles to acquiring these skills that are faced by clinical staff: most significantly, the daunting quantity of information and the competing pressures on their time.

Enliven and illuminate key points.

Expand your argument.

Provide a bridge to a key point.

Here are some ways of presenting evidence in your assignment.

1 **Brief mention:** You briefly refer to a source; here is an example from Dan's assignment on homelessness:

> At the end of March 2020, Dame Louise Casey began what is now known as the 'Everyone In' rough sleepers' initiative (House of Commons Library, Briefing Paper, 2021).

2 **Summary:** You take a large item, perhaps a whole article or book chapter, and reduce it to one or two lines. For example, you might want to produce some background context:

> Casey discussed the way that the clients using homelessness services are changing, together with the support infrastructure. She concluded that it was vital that health services and homeless organisations collaborate closely, to ensure the safety of both homeless people and homeless workers alike (House of Commons Housing, Communities and Local Government Committee, 18 January 2021, HC 309 Q268).

You summarise a key take-away point from a source that is relevant to your argument.

3 **Paraphrase:** You demonstrate your understanding of the topic by rephrasing the key concepts in your own words. But, of course, you also acknowledge your source. For instance, in Olivia's assignment about the destruction of coral reefs:

Wilkinson and Salvat (2011) investigate Hardin's use of the term 'tragedy of the commons' and its subsequent history in relation to coastal depredation. They suggest that natural resources have continued to decline. Although the events are indeed 'tragic', they are based on factors that require scientific, but also political and even moral considerations.

4 **Quotation:** Use a **short quotation** when you want to analyse or comment on the exact words of a source, an individual or a scholar. Here are two examples:

Regan's ominous line: 'I pray you, father, being weak, **seem so**' (Shakespeare, *King Lear*, act 2, scene 4, line 10, emphasis added), is pivotal. The idea of 'seeming', of appearance, in the play will occupy the next section of this essay.

The independent Parliamentary Select Committee was extremely concerned about the impact of COVID-19 on the homeless. When Dame Louise Casey was a witness, she said that there was a level of 'relentlessness, fear and fatigue' among the homeless organisations (House of Commons Housing, Communities and Local Government Committee, 18 January 2021, HC 309 Q246). It became clear from other evidence that this was no exaggeration.

Your quotation might be short, or extended. **Extended quotations** must be used with care, and they must have a clear point. If you cannot build on each quotation and add something substantial to your argument, it will simply look like filler, demonstrating a lack of analysis.

The NHA (National Housing Association) produced important evidence to the Committee on the government's emergency funding for rough sleepers during the pandemic. Although this money was welcome, it did not take full account of the impact of the pandemic on support services. The NHA stated that:

Dan is using the long quote to help build his argument.

> Support services also report significant levels of staff absence due to illness and self-isolation (15–25%), which brings additional costs when agency staff are needed to replace them or existing staff are redeployed, incurring administrative costs. Some organisations are modelling for absences of up to 70%, which would make some smaller organisations no longer financially viable. Without extra financial support, some services may need to close, meaning a return to rough sleeping for many and increased costs in healthcare, policing, social care, housing and welfare. (National Housing Association, 2021, p. 4)

One key point here is that the crisis demonstrated how different services are interrelated. When one service was impacted by COVID-19, it had a knock-on effect on other services, and consequently, government policy was thrown off course.

A word on tense and style when you reference

In the examples above, the Social Policy student is writing about the literature in the past tense. He might write: 'Casey (2021) described the variety of people involved.' The same sentence could equally be written in the present tense: 'Casey (2021) describes the variety of people involved.' Either tense is acceptable, but be consistent.

In some subject areas, the name of the individual author being referenced is not quite so relevant, and so the reference goes at the end of the sentence. Consequently, a Construction Management student might write: 'A second article forcefully illustrated the need for regular on-site inspection (Hegarty, 2019).' When you reference the literature, the style will depend on what is accepted practice in your subject discipline. Always be aware of the literature in your subject and ask your lecturers for guidance.

A checklist on how to show your evidence

▸ **Follow departmental guidelines:** Your department will usually have guidance on whether quotation in the text is encouraged and how short and long quotations should be used.

▸ **Quote for a reason:** Every single quotation has to make a point. Ask yourself: 'What exactly is the function of this quotation? How does it help me to communicate my argument?' The point that an author makes may support your argument, but an author's individual words are not necessarily special. Often, if you summarise and give a reference – e.g. (National Housing Association, 2021, p. 4) – this is more effective than simply shoving a quotation into your text. If you are not actively using a quotation, you are wasting words.

▶ **Have a system:** Every time you put a quotation or paraphrase into your writing, you need to know exactly where it came from so that you can go back and check for accuracy, and to avoid plagiarism. This is where using electronic referencing systems can be so helpful.

▶ **Quote exactly:** If you DO quote, use the exact words including punctuation marks. You must avoid plagiarism. If you know that a punctuation mark or spelling in the original is incorrect, there is a convention for indicating this. Use 'sic' (Latin for 'thus') in square brackets. Here's an example:

> She wrote that 'Apple's latest iOS software is way more secure than Andriod [sic] is offering'.

▶ **Avoid being too obvious:** In the quote below, the student has just repeated academic research without adding anything at all, so that the result is not a fresh insight, but a cliché:

> Young people may have experienced loneliness during lockdown, as the Mental Health Foundation (2021) argues.

- **Be restrained:** It's much more effective to use a small number of precise quotations than to add lots of quotes, as though you were just tipping an assortment of vegetables into a pot and hoping for a tasty soup!

- **Avoid the lonely quotation:** It will sit there, at the end of your paragraph, with no chance to make a meaningful contribution. And it will not impress your tutor.

The use of references is one area where everybody can learn by reading expert authors in their field. There's more about citing and referencing in *Referencing and Understanding Plagiarism* in this series.

Your numeric evidence

If you are using numeric (quantitative) data in your assignments, and presenting tables, graphs and charts, signal their arrival by giving the table or figure number. When you're drawing on figures to support your assignment, the reader must know where to look within your text for the original data. For instance:

Further predictor variables are given in Table 1.2.

The differences between the two approaches are displayed in Figure 3.1, below.

Your department may have specific guidance on the use of quantitative data, figures and tables, and you can also find useful advice on the web.

This chapter has discussed some of the conventions for presenting evidence in an assignment. Now let's look at ways to communicate effectively with your reader.

As you go through your course, you will be encouraged to develop your own academic writing style. In this chapter, you will learn some of the key skills for improving your ability to communicate in writing.

Be aware of your writing persona

Present a version of yourself

When your tutors read your work, they want to read the thoughts of a student who follows the conventions, argues carefully and has a lively mind. It's helpful to develop a 'persona', an academic character you can project through your writing. As always, the specific qualities of your persona will relate to what is expected in your subject discipline.

Write for the reader

As well as creating your own writing persona, you need to be aware of the reader. You are not just writing for your tutor. In fact, you are writing for your school; there may be a second marker and, later on, an external examiner. So avoid making assumptions about their familiarity with your assignment question or with you as a student. You might want to imagine your reader as the 'general educated reader', with some knowledge of your discipline. In academic writing, it's a good idea to build up an imaginary **dialogue** with this general educated reader.

Create a dialogue with your reader

Try to imagine a real person reading your text: smiling, frowning, getting involved and reacting to your words. You're going to encourage them to see your arguments positively, to enjoy your style and to consider you as a member of an academic community.

To help create this dialogue, you can use various devices to organise the text. Then the reader can understand it better and will be more receptive to your argument.

Here are four ways to create a dialogue with your reader:

1 Show your structure
See Part 3 for how to develop well-sequenced paragraphs and consistent headings.

2 Use formatting

Here are some useful typographical features to help structure your pages. Make sure they are in the house style approved by your department:

▶ headings (if allowed by your department)
▶ use of bold/italic
▶ lists
▶ bullet points if appropriate
▶ numbering
▶ indenting.

All these make it easy for the reader to grasp the shape of your assignment and to work through it as efficiently as possible.

3 Use reader-based prose

Readers want to get a sense of your work as quickly as possible. Right from the first page, they will be looking for information about how your assignment works. If they get no clues, they may either get annoyed, or start making their own assumptions about how you have tackled the assignment.

It helps your marker if you use some of the key phrases from the assignment brief. Echo back important vocabulary, as well as using your own language. So, if your assignment asks you to use 'one of the following psychological or sociological theoretical models', position the phrase 'psychological model' or 'sociological model' near the beginning, and be explicit about which model you are using and why.

4 Use pronouns to signal your connection with the reader

One aspect of your writing identity is to make claims about yourself as well as your argument. When you use *I, me, we* or *one*, you are claiming to have a connection with your reader, and claiming some authority, which may or may not be appropriate. So do be careful how you use the pronouns 'we' and 'I'.

Use of 'I'

The use of the first-person pronoun 'I' depends very much on your subject discipline, the approach taken in your department and also the individual assignment. It is discouraged by many tutors as being too informal, especially in your first year of study. Additionally, a more impersonal style (known as the 'passive voice') is normal in science-based subjects. For example:

The *p*-values for each group were obtained through the Anderson-Darling test. (Undergraduate BEng.)

This particular section of the transcript was considered challenging to analyse. (BSc Applied Linguistics)

However, there are two areas where the use of 'I' is normal. First, let's take the sentence:

> I found this section of my conversation with the patient especially difficult to analyse. (BSc Nursing)

This usage would be appropriate if you had been asked to write a reflective essay. For more on this topic, see *Reflective Writing* in this series.

Second, in qualitative research, tutors will want their students to interpret real-life settings and situations that are not subject to 'objective fact'. Consequently, reporting a personal viewpoint using 'I' is sometimes appropriate. There is more about this in Chapter 13 on academic voice, including an example of how it can work. If in doubt, check with your tutor to be sure about appropriate style.

Use of 'we'

The use of the plural pronoun 'we' is common in many disciplines but **only** in certain circumstances. For instance, only when the student is able to demonstrate real authority and some deep subject knowledge; *possibly* in a Master's or in a PhD dissertation:

> From all this evidence, we can see that coral reefs must be actively managed in order to prevent further rapid degradation. (MSc Environmental Science)

Additionally, at undergraduate level, if you have been working as a team, and are asked to reflect on group dynamics, 'we' might be appropriate. Here is an example from a reflective journal.

Positive example:

I learned that when the team was working on the project – to a deadline and under pressure – we did not guard against the potential power of 'groupthink'. So we let one strong-minded individual take over our decision-making process, and then later we regretted it. (BSc Construction Management)

However, and especially at undergraduate level, if you fail to provide compelling evidence and back up your claim, some general statements will seem a little naive to your marker.

Example to avoid:

We all know that social media means that many young people are living their inner lives very differently from those of adults. (BSc Digital Marketing and Social Media)

Our guidance: only use 'we' if you are **absolutely certain** that this style is going to be appropriate in its context and, most importantly, acceptable to your tutors.

Writing in a second language

Using 'I' and other pronouns can be confusing. It is doubly confusing for students writing in a second language. You may be expected to write very differently in your country of study from how you wrote back home. There may be variations between what individual lecturers suggest and between academics in the same discipline across different institutions. As always, be guided by your tutor.

This chapter examined how to make the initial connection with the reader. In the next chapter, learn how to use a technique called 'academic voice' to explain and clarify your argument.

Finding your academic voice

You've been reading about:

▶ establishing your line of argument

▶ finding and using evidence

▶ constructing the overall shape and the paragraphs and sentences of your assignment.

But there's another ingredient. In order to communicate with your reader, it helps to express your argument in a special style known as 'academic voice'. You will almost certainly have been using some academic voice techniques before now, perhaps without knowing the term.

What is academic voice?

Your academic voice is the way you, as part of the academic community, use certain words to present yourself to the reader. The techniques include how you paraphrase and use quotations, and your 'stance', which partly means the ability to express judgements and opinions in your writing. These techniques appear in all disciplines and academics use them constantly.

When you use your academic voice, you are:

- Demonstrating that you understand the subject, and the task you have been asked to achieve.
- Bringing forward compelling and well-assembled evidence.
- Showing that you have an analytical and critical approach to previous research. For instance, you might be able to point out limitations in a previous methodology or, indeed, the constraints on your own research for a dissertation.
- Presenting your own evidence-based viewpoint, when it is appropriate.

Use these techniques carefully, and you will give your writing more authority and credibility.

So what does academic voice actually look like? Here is a student writing about their work-based project:

Another factor to be considered is diversity in teams. As far back as 2014, writers were suggesting that millennials were natural change agents, because they had been born into a time of rapid change (Farrelly, 2014) The team in question only contained one millennial, the researcher. Consequently, the management might well consider having a greater focus on diversity in order to effectively drive through change.

An idea from the literature.

The student applies the idea from the literature.

The student's voice shines through.

How do you communicate your arguments authentically? We will now show you some tools for communicating your argument using your academic voice. When you have learned how to use these tools, they can make a major and positive change to your writing style.

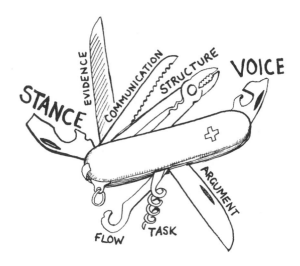

Examples of academic voice

1 Steering your reader with directives

Directives gently guide readers towards your viewpoint. They are common when writing about research, and are a standard element of science writing. In the following examples, the directive is in **bold**:

> **It can be seen** from the values of the variance in Table 1.1 **that** the data of Engineer 1 are less scattered and varied than that of Engineer 2. (Undergraduate BEng.)

> **It is important to note that** UK construction industry fatalities actually increased during 2019/20 (Tyler, 2020, p. 13). (BSc Construction Management)

2 Framing references to indicate a point of view

You reinforce your argument through evidence, often researched from previous writers. This is one of the best-known academic skills, but quotations and paraphrases can be used more subtly than you might imagine. You can express a certain amount of approval or concern for the sources you cite, depending on your choice of words.

In this example, Ofcom is the UK telecoms regulator. We have emboldened the influencing word or phrase in each quotation.

Using your academic voice to gently support an argument

Note the choice of verbs in these two examples:

Ofcom research (2017) **suggests** that more than one in ten children aged 3–4 have their own tablet.

Ofcom research (2017) **reveals** that young children's language development could be affected by social media. For instance, the research **points out** that more than 65% of children aged 3–4 regularly used a tablet.

A slightly positive nudge to your reader, implying that the research has drawn back a curtain.

Using your voice to be neutral about your source

Notice how important the choice of verb is to convey neutrality:

Research by Ofcom (2014) **states** that more than one in ten children aged 3–4 have their own tablet or other device. Personal ownership of devices by young children is a recent development.

3 Expressing caution

Most of the time, your tutor will want you to put forward your own evidence-based views and comment on the views of academics in your field. Your comments are expected to be thoughtful, cautiously critical and not wildly speculative. Your tutor will

not want you to overstate your case and, especially at undergraduate level, it is better to appear slightly tentative rather than overassertive.

So you might consider using a convention called **hedging**. This simply means using a phrase to express caution, such as 'It is possible that …' or 'Probably …'. This signals to the marker that you realise it is difficult to be completely sure of all the facts; you are making the best judgement you can, based on the evidence. You may not be completely certain about what you are writing and, in fact, some markers will give you credit for expressing a nuanced viewpoint. The phrases below in bold are all hedges.

It is likely that the respondent is still without work.
Data collected so far **suggest that** satisfaction levels remain high.
In some circumstances patients may make a surprising recovery.
The conflicts between the two communities over cultural differences make **it seem probable that** the cause of the violence was primarily social, rather than religious.

Here are some more examples of how your voice, the choice of phrasing, expresses caution:

> Ofcom research (2017) **claims** that more than 78% of children aged 3–4 had access to a tablet at home.
>
> Research by Ofcom (2017) **estimated** that more than 78% of children aged 3–4 had access to a tablet at home. **However, it should be noted** that this question addressed access to a device and not the frequency of use (Ofcom, 2017, p. 22).

Note the choice of verb, conveying caution.

Hedging practice does vary between disciplines, so talk to your tutor or read examples of the literature in your subject area if you are unsure.

Warning: avoid over-promoting your argument

Pushing your argument too strongly can cause problems. Here's an example:

> Ofcom research (2017) **demonstrates convincingly** that UK parents are massively concerned by the amount of time their children spend watching television.

The use of the word *massive* is an exaggeration and inappropriate, even if you have a lot of evidence, and the word *convincingly* appears presumptuous. Convincing to whom? So be careful and measured with your language and avoid using superlatives, e.g. *an enormous effect* or *a huge advance*. Instead, support your argument with good quality evidence and sensible, reasoned logic.

4 Using academic voice to shape your argument

Here, we use the example of an Education student writing about dyslexia to show how academic voice can help to shape your argument.

Proposing an argument

Genetic studies **suggest** that certain genes are in some way involved in dyslexia (Bishop, 2015). It **seems probable** that dyslexia has a hereditary component. But only a component: Thambirajah (2010, p. 303) **indicates** that the genes responsible for dyslexia are also the genes responsible for normal variations in reading ability. Consequently, it is difficult to say to what extent genes alone might be responsible for dyslexia.

A hedge: you are keeping your options open.

You are highlighting previous research in order to make a point about how research perspectives change over time.

Countering an argument

The visual processing theories **so prominent** 20 years ago are now less popular but they still have their adherents. However, more **recent research** (Williams, 2015) **indicates** that many children diagnosed with dyslexia have perfectly good eyesight, which seems to cast doubt on visual processing theories.

An appropriate note of caution.

Conceding a point

There are many examples of the way that visual processing theories seem to illuminate the understanding of dyslexia (Cheng et al., 2018). **However**, **some** brain scanning research appears to demonstrate that dyslexia is primarily concerned with deficits in phonological processing (Boets et al., 2013).

You are being careful; claiming only limited knowledge.

Reconciling several viewpoints

Indeed, much of the evidence implies that dyslexia may not have one simple cause, as environmental, genetic (hereditary) and individual brain factors are equally involved.

A gentle hedge, showing caution; at undergraduate level at least, you are not claiming to have read every single scrap of evidence.

Academic voice in practice-based assignments

In standard written academic assignments such as essays, your tone and your academic voice will be pretty consistent. However, suppose that you are writing a reflective assignment on workplace practice. You're being asked to combine your personal experience with theoretical material from the literature. Does your academic voice alter?

The answer is probably yes! In these cases, striking an appropriate tone can feel even more challenging. You may be switching between discussing the literature in a more 'traditional' academic voice, and reflecting on your practical experiences in the first person, for instance 'I think ...', 'I feel ...' or 'I observed ...'. This might feel strange at first, but you will become more confident as you attempt more of these kinds of assignments. Reading reflective accounts in journals or books will help, too.

Here is a short example to show how you might move between two subtly different voices in a work-based assignment that combines theory with practice. Pay attention to how the discussion of theory leads into a first-person commentary on the student's work placement. Referring back to the theory again at the end creates a strong link between the two.

The paragraph starts with theory.

Gosling (2016) questioned whether it makes more sense to be focusing on leadership of continuity rather than on the leadership of change. By focusing on continuity, sustaining a sense of identity and purpose despite continuous change, leaders can provide stability. And through stability, people negotiate their place as workplace changes unfold. Applying this approach to my own organisation, I argued that we should not pull all five different change programmes into one future vision; instead, we should focus on helping our workforce to feel more stable and more secure through a time of continuous change. This might allow them to bond more effectively with the organisation (Gosling, 2008)

Transition from theory to practice.

Link back to theory. So the paragraph moves from theory, to practice, and then back to theory.

Summary: showing your argument

If you use the tools above, respond to feedback from your lecturers and keep practising your writing, you will be able to build up your own individual academic voice. You'll be showing how your thoughts and ideas mesh with, and are built on, existing knowledge.

Having read Part 4, you should be better able to express your viewpoints and use some of the techniques that academics expect in assignments. Part 5 will show you how to give your work a professional polish.

FINALISING YOUR ARGUMENT

As you edit and polish your work, you will be trying to make your writing as interesting and easy to read as possible, while ensuring that you have answered the question, presented a convincing case and observed academic conventions.

Editing and redrafting

The redrafting and editing stages **must be all about the reader**. As you look over your work, find ways to distance yourself from it as much as possible:

- Leave a few days between the writing and editing stages to allow yourself to look at your work with fresh eyes.
- Print off your essay to do your editing, preferably in a different font from the one you have used to type it, to make it look different.

- Check your flow by reading the whole essay from start to finish. Many people edit as they go along and never actually do an entire read-through, which means they fail to see the whole picture, making it hard to prevent repetition or identify structural issues.
- Keep anything you cut out in a separate document called 'Scrap' or similar, just in case you ever need it again. This will also make it less painful to trim your work!
- When editing, try to imagine you are a marker picking this essay up for the very first time. How well have the key messages been communicated, along with the evidence that supports them?

For more on editing and proofreading, see *Writing for University* in this series.

Make a good impression on your reader: some guidelines

Do you know the research about the first 30 seconds of an interview? That's the key period when interviewers tend to make up their minds about the candidate. We think something similar happens when the marker picks up your assignment or when it pops up on their computer screen. They will be scanning your essay to see if you have observed the following standard academic conventions.

Guidelines for standard academic conventions

Conventions	What they don't want to see
Correct completion of the top sheet, e.g. module name, student ID, etc.	A top sheet with obvious details missing.
Clear paragraphs: they may read the first and last sentences of paragraphs during this initial scan	Whole pages with no paragraph breaks, or suspiciously short paragraphs that suggest underdeveloped ideas.
Numbered pages	Unnumbered pages: a disaster if the assignment is printed off and it looks unprofessional.
Some variety of sentences	Very long sentences, which are hard to follow.
Consistent academic referencing	No referencing, which could lead to the student being penalised for plagiarism.
Clarity of expression	Muddled use of language.
Clearly developed ideas	Unoriginal ideas: no marker wants a whole pile of scripts that all say the same thing, or that aren't really saying anything at all!
Awareness of marking criteria	Evidence that the student has no idea how the assignment will be marked.

Some **specific departmental conventions** your marker will scan for include the following:

▶ **Specific referencing system:** Have you been consistent? And there might be more than one system within the department.
▶ **Specific layout guidelines:** For example, do they allow the use of headings in essays?
▶ **Particular language preferences:** Can you demonstrate that you use the language of the subject with confidence?

As a student, one of your jobs is to use a professional writer's approach. Taking time and care with the final draft is one of those professional touches.

Conclusion

In this book, we have suggested various approaches to help you form and communicate your argument. We have also offered some practical tips to help you:

▶ Understand the task (**Chapters 1, 2, 3** and **Part 5**).
▶ Find information and explore ideas (**Chapters 3** and **4**).
▶ Ask critical questions (**Chapters 4** and **5**).
▶ Collect and present appropriate evidence (**Chapters 5** and **6**).
▶ Build your argument (**Chapters 6, 7** and **8**).

- Give your reader a take-home message about your argument (**Chapters 6, 7** and **8**).
- Plan a logical structure (**Chapters 6, 7** and **10**).
- Move towards valid conclusions supported by the evidence (**Chapter 11**).
- Write with an awareness of the whole assignment, paragraphs and sentence structure (**Chapters 8** and **9**).
- Think about your reader (**Chapter 12**). ← *Also throughout the book!*
- Develop your own academic voice (**Chapter 13**).
- Be aware of departmental conventions (**Chapter 11** and **Part 5**).

Two take-home messages

We have encouraged you to give your reader a memorable take-home message about your argument.

But there is another message. If you can communicate clearly with your reader and show them that you understand academic writing conventions, they will respond positively. So, your second message to your reader is that you have thought about effective communication in academic writing.

If you continually develop the skills in this book, these key writing principles will become a natural part of your academic toolkit.

WHERE'S YOUR ARGUMENT?

References

Coonan E (2020) *Where's Your Evidence?* London: Red Globe Press.

Godfrey J (2014) *Reading and Making Notes* (2nd edn). Basingstoke: Palgrave Macmillan.

Godfrey J (2016) *Writing for University* (2nd edn). London: Palgrave.

Godwin J (2019) *Planning Your Essay* (3rd edn). London: Red Globe Press.

Williams K (2022) *Getting Critical* (3rd edn). London: Bloomsbury.

Williams K and Davis M (2017) *Referencing and Understanding Plagiarism* (2nd edn). London: Palgrave.

Williams K and Reid M (2011) *Time Management*. Basingstoke: Palgrave Macmillan.

Williams K, Woolliams M and Spiro J (2020) *Reflective Writing* (2nd edn). London: Bloomsbury.

Useful sources

Hyland K (2012) Undergraduate Understandings: stance and voice in final year reports. In K Hyland and C Sancho Guinda (eds) *Stance and Voice in Written Academic Genres*. Basingstoke: Palgrave Macmillan, pp. 134–50.

Pears K and Shields G (2022) *Cite Them Right: The essential referencing guide* (12th edn). London: Bloomsbury.

Index